TEACHING STARTS

IN THE HEART

TEACHING STARTS IN THE HEART: A TEACHER'S PLANNER

Teaching Starts In The Heart:
A Teacher's Planner
Created & Published 2021
by S. Mabley of
2wa Scoops ENT, LLC
ISBN: 978-1-7373158-5-8

This Planner Belongs To:

_____

Welcome to your new year!

NAME
SCHOOL
YEAR
GRADE
PHONE

OTHER IMPORTANT INFORMATION

Goals

SHORT TERM PERSONAL

LONG TERM PERSONAL

SHORT TERM PROFESSIONAL

LONG TERM PROFESSIONAL

Smart Goals

S
(specific)

M
(measurable)

A
(attainable)

R
(relevant)

T
(time-based)

Even though you're already a teacher...

NEVER STOP LEARNING

BIRTHDAYS

JANUARY _____

FEBRUARY _____

MARCH   _____

APRIL   _____

MAY   _____

JUNE   _____

JULY   _____

AUGUST   _____

SEPTEMBER _____

OCTOBER _____

NOVEMBER _____

DECEMBER _____

2021-2022 School Calendar

August 2021

Su	Mo	Tu	We	Th	Fr	Sa
1	2	3	4	5	6	7
8	9	10	11	12	13	14
15	16	17	18	19	20	21
22	23	24	25	26	27	28
29	30	31				

September 2021

Su	Mo	Tu	We	Th	Fr	Sa
			1	2	3	4
5	6	7	8	9	10	11
12	13	14	15	16	17	18
19	20	21	22	23	24	25
26	27	28	29	30		

October 2021

Su	Mo	Tu	We	Th	Fr	Sa
					1	2
3	4	5	6	7	8	9
10	11	12	13	14	15	16
17	18	19	20	21	22	23
24	25	26	27	28	29	30
31						

November 2021

Su	Mo	Tu	We	Th	Fr	Sa
	1	2	3	4	5	6
7	8	9	10	11	12	13
14	15	16	17	18	19	20
21	22	23	24	25	26	27
28	29	30				

December 2021

Su	Mo	Tu	We	Th	Fr	Sa
			1	2	3	4
5	6	7	8	9	10	11
12	13	14	15	16	17	18
19	20	21	22	23	24	25
26	27	28	29	30	31	

January 2022

Su	Mo	Tu	We	Th	Fr	Sa
						1
2	3	4	5	6	7	8
9	10	11	12	13	14	15
16	17	18	19	20	21	22
23	24	25	26	27	28	29
30	31					

February 2022

Su	Mo	Tu	We	Th	Fr	Sa
		1	2	3	4	5
6	7	8	9	10	11	12
13	14	15	16	17	18	19
20	21	22	23	24	25	26
27	28					

March 2022

Su	Mo	Tu	We	Th	Fr	Sa
		1	2	3	4	5
6	7	8	9	10	11	12
13	14	15	16	17	18	19
20	21	22	23	24	25	26
27	28	29	30	31		

April 2022

Su	Mo	Tu	We	Th	Fr	Sa
					1	2
3	4	5	6	7	8	9
10	11	12	13	14	15	16
17	18	19	20	21	22	23
24	25	26	27	28	29	30

May 2022

Su	Mo	Tu	We	Th	Fr	Sa
1	2	3	4	5	6	7
8	9	10	11	12	13	14
15	16	17	18	19	20	21
22	23	24	25	26	27	28
29	30	31				

June 2022

Su	Mo	Tu	We	Th	Fr	Sa
			1	2	3	4
5	6	7	8	9	10	11
12	13	14	15	16	17	18
19	20	21	22	23	24	25
26	27	28	29	30		

July 2022

Su	Mo	Tu	We	Th	Fr	Sa
					1	2
3	4	5	6	7	8	9
10	11	12	13	14	15	16
17	18	19	20	21	22	23
24	25	26	27	28	29	30
31						

Federal Holidays

Sep 6, 2021 - Labor Day
Oct. 11, 2021-Columbus Day
Nov. 11, 2021-Veterans' Day
Nov. 25, 2021-Thanksgiving

Dec. 24, 2021 - Christmas Eve
Dec. 25, 2021 - Christmas Day
Dec. 31, 2021 - New Year's Eve
Jan 1, 2022 - New Year's Day

Jan 17, 2022 - Martin L. King Day
Feb. 21, 2022 - Presidents' Day
May 30, 2022 - Memorial Day
June 19, 2022 - Juneteenth
July 4, 2022 - Independence Day

Important Dates

Teacher

Noun. /Tee.chur/

An educational superhero, superb multi-tasker & fixer of problems. An individual who loves to inspire and encourage.

A Teacher's Prayer

LORD, enable me to teach with *wisdom,* for I help to shape the mind; *truth,* for I help to shape the *conscience;* for I help to shape the *future.* Empower me to teach with *love,* for I help to shape the  **WORLD!!!**

WEEKLY PLAN

1ST *Week*

2ND *Week*

3RD *Week*

4TH *Week*

5TH *Week*

A TEACHER'S JOURNAL

AUGUST 2021

HAVE A GREAT YEAR!!!

THUR	FRI	SAT	MONTHLY CHECK-IN
5	6	7	**Were you ready for school to start back?** (JOURNAL HERE) _____ _____ _____ _____
12	13	14	
19	20	21	**Take-Care-of-Yourself Projects**
26	27	28	

WELCOME BACK!

WEEKLY PLAN

1ST Week
_____
_____
_____

2ND Week
_____
_____
_____

3RD Week
_____
_____
_____

4TH Week
_____
_____
_____

5TH Week
_____
_____
_____

A TEACHER'S JOURNAL

SEPTEMBER 2021

RELAX AT HOME

THUR	FRI	SAT
2	3	4
9	10	11
16	17	18
23	24	25
30		

MONTHLY CHECK-IN

First month going ok?
(JOURNAL HERE)

_____
_____
_____
_____
_____

Do-It-For-Yourself List

DON'T FORGET TO WIND DOWN

WEEKLY PLAN

1ST Week
_____
_____
_____

2ND Week
_____
_____
_____

3RD Week
_____
_____
_____

4TH Week
_____
_____
_____

5TH Week
_____
_____
_____

A TEACHER'S JOURNAL

OCTOBER 2021

ALSO SHOW YOUR SCHOOL SPIRIT!!!

THUR	FRI	SAT
	1	2
7	8	9
14	15	16
21	22	23
28	29	30

MONTHLY CHECK-IN

Have you taken any time for yourself lately?
(JOURNAL HERE)
_____
_____
_____
_____
_____

Things I can't wait to teach:

TAKE PRIDE IN ALL YOU DO

WEEKLY PLAN

1ST Week

2ND Week

3RD Week

4TH Week

5TH Week

A TEACHER'S JOURNAL

NOVEMBER 2021

Remain humble & grateful

give thanks

SUN	MON	TUES	WED
		1	2	3
7 (DAYLIGHT SAVINGS TIME)	8	9	10
14	15	16	17
21	22	23	24
28	29	30	

Thanksgiving

Notes

WEEKLY PLAN

1ST *Week*
_____
_____
_____

2ND *Week*
_____
_____
_____

3RD *Week*
_____
_____
_____

4TH *Week*
_____
_____
_____

5TH *Week*
_____
_____
_____

A TEACHER'S JOURNAL

WEEKLY PLAN

1ST Week

2ND Week

3RD Week

4TH Week

5TH Week

A TEACHER'S JOURNAL

JANUARY 2022

MAKE NEW YEAR RESOLUTIONS

SUN	MON	TUES	WED
2	3	4	5
9	10	11	12
16	17 *Martin Luther King Jr. Day*	18	19
23	24	25	26
30	31		

Notes
_____
_____
_____
_____
_____
_____
_____
_____
_____
_____
_____

JANUARY 2022

HALF-WAY THERE!!!!!!

THUR	FRI	SAT
		1 happy new year
6	7	8
13	14	15
20	21	22
27	28	29

MONTHLY REFLECTION

List your new year's goals:
(JOURNAL HERE)

_____
_____
_____
_____

Your Goals For Your Students:

REMAIN HELPFUL & KIND

WEEKLY PLAN

1ST *Week*
_____
_____
_____

2ND *Week*
_____
_____
_____

3RD *Week*
_____
_____
_____

4TH *Week*
_____
_____
_____

5TH *Week*
_____
_____
_____

A TEACHER'S JOURNAL

FEBRUARY 2022

LOVE YOURSELF, YOU DESERVE IT

SUN	MON	TUES	WED
Notes	BLACK HISTORY MONTH	1	2 Groundhog's Day
	6	7	8	9
	13 Happy Galentine's Day	14 Happy Valentine's Day	15	16
	20	21 President's Day	22	23
	27	28		

WEEKLY PLAN

1ST Week
___
___
___

2ND Week
___
___
___

3RD Week
___
___
___

4TH Week
___
___
___

5TH Week
___
___
___

A TEACHER'S JOURNAL

MARCH 2022

SOMETIMES, IT TAKES GETTING DOWN TO THEIR LEVEL...

SUN	MON	TUES	WED
		1	2
6	7	8	9
13 *Daylight Savings Time Begins*	14	15	16
20 *Spring Starts*	21	22	23
27	28	29	30

Notes

MARCH 2022

... FOR THEM TO BETTER UNDERSTAND.

THUR	FRI	SAT
3	4	5
10	11	12
17	18	19
24	25	26
31		

MONTHLY CHECK-IN

In teaching, what's the best advice you've ever been given?
(JOURNAL HERE)
_____
_____
_____
_____

How will you continue to bring your best self to your career?

THESE KIDS NEED YOU!

WEEKLY PLAN

1ST Week

2ND Week

3RD Week

4TH Week

5TH Week

A TEACHER'S JOURNAL

WEEKLY PLAN

1ST Week

2ND Week

3RD Week

4TH Week

5TH Week

A TEACHER'S JOURNAL

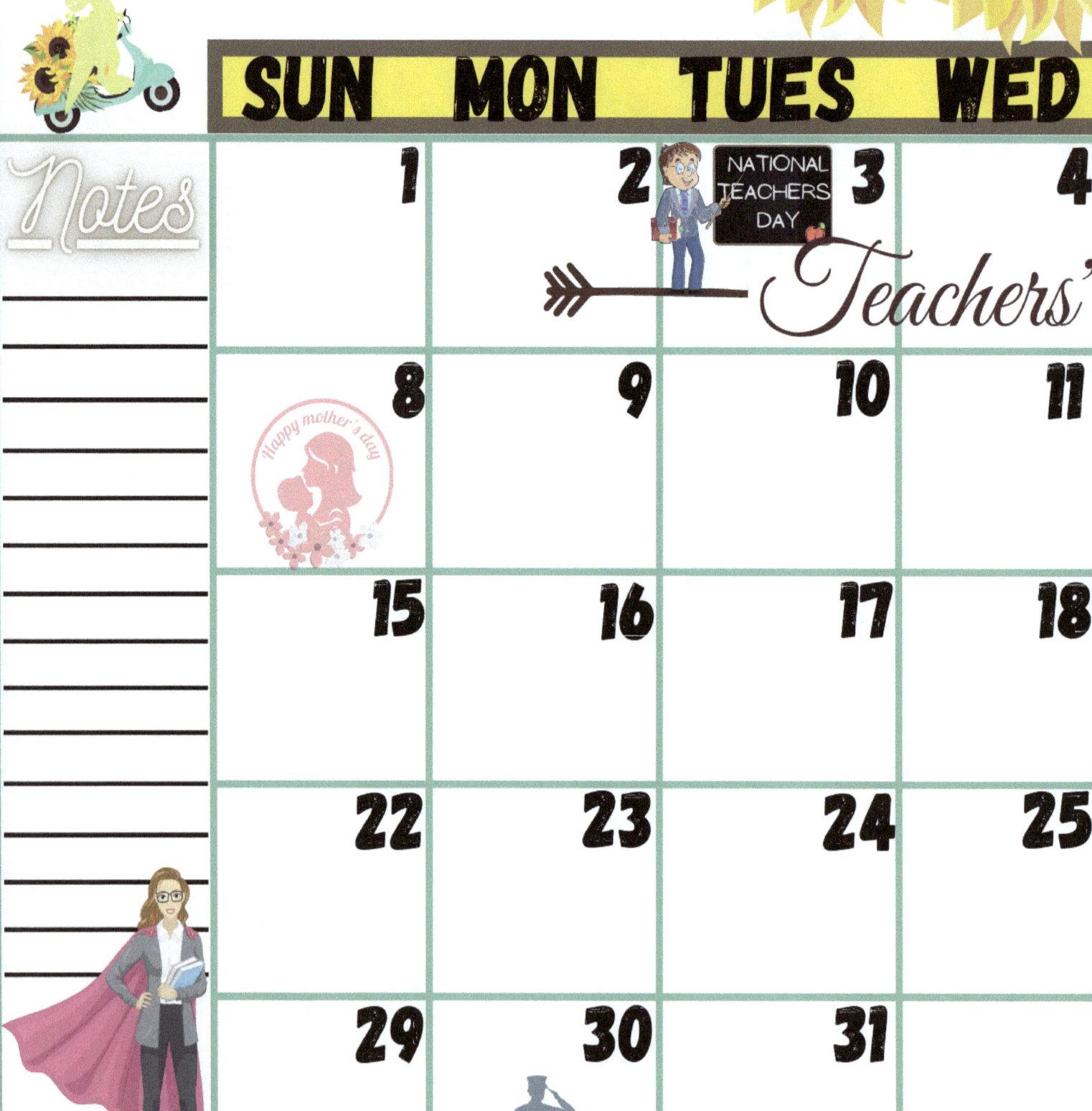

MAY 2022

Help them be as determined as you are!!!

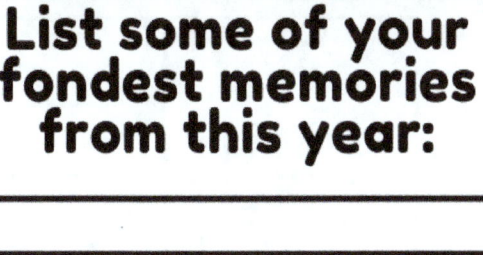

THUR	FRI	SAT
5	6	7
Week →		
12	13	14
19	20	21
26	27	28

CONGRATS Grads!!!

MONTHLY CHECK-IN

List some of your fondest memories from this year:
_____
_____
_____
_____

MORE MEMORIES:

GIVE YOURSELF PRAISE!!!

WEEKLY PLAN

1ST Week

2ND Week

3RD Week

4TH Week

5TH Week

A TEACHER'S JOURNAL

A TEACHER'S JOURNAL

Assessment Record

PERIOD_____

STUDENT	PROJECT												

Assessment Record

PERIOD _____

STUDENT	PROJECT												

Assessment Record

PERIOD_____

STUDENT	PROJECT										

Assessment Record

PERIOD _____

STUDENT	PROJECT											

Assessment Record

PERIOD_____

STUDENT	PROJECT											

Assessment Record

PERIOD_____

PROJECT

STUDENT

Assessment Record

PERIOD_____

STUDENT	PROJECT												

Thank You

For those countless late nights you stay up to finish grading papers. For the amount of sacrifice it takes to be there and be present, no matter what.

For your enormous heart and amazing generosity, we thank you, we praise you, we salute you!!!

With love,
2woScoopsPublished.com

A fun way to get to know your students

Name: Date:

BACK 2 SCHOOL

What I wish my teacher knew about me

What makes me happy:

Things that worry me:

What helps me learn:

Things I find easy:

Things I find hard:

What makes me sad:

DISTANCE EDUCATION
Tips for teaching at home

PREPARE IN ADVANCE

If you expect to teach remotely in the near future, look at the curriculum in advance and prepare lessons for the weeks ahead.

Opt for content that's easily accessible online, in a variety of mediums.

SCHEDULE STUDENT CHECK-IN TIMES

Set time when you and your students can touch base and have them prepare questions they had during the exercises.

Make use of video conference tools that allow for multiple people to dial in.

SET UP A WORK ZONE

Set up a comfortable, well-lit area and designate it for work.

Avoid working from the couch or bed - when it is time to relax your brain might find it hard to shut off work thoughts.

CREATE AN ONLINE QUIZ

Check in on your students' learning progress through online methods.

Use a tool like Google Forms to make an online quiz any student can fill out with their device.

OVER-COMMUNICATE

Set out your expectations clearly in all relevant communication channels.

Make sure students know exactly where to receive their assignments, submit their work, or ask questions.

BE FLEXIBLE

Be empathetic of the home situation of students as some may not have available adult supervision or reliable internet.

If students need special support, be open to their unique needs.

Check out other great and useful creations by

2woscoopspublished.com

REALLY GREAT FRIENDS
Children's book that portrays the unbiased and selfless way children view their peers who are different from them. For children & adults

Learn Cursive Practice Workbook
Workbook that teaches cursive writing and reading. Includes full alphabet and words in cursive, silly sentences to read and practice, and fun pictures to color!

2021-2022 Student Planner
Self-esteem and self-awareness boosting planner/agenda, with space for assignments and life advice at every page turn! For students of all ages.

CHECK OUT OTHER GREAT AND USEFUL CREATIONS BY

2woscoopspublished.com

Lil Girlfriends Pick a Career

Coloring book showing lil black and brown girls that they can be anything they want to be, with the beautiful hair (crown) they've been blessed with.

The B.A.P/BIG Planner

For the short woman, the tall woman, the do-it-all woman! Inspirational, motivational, empowering 18-month planner/journal.
For women.

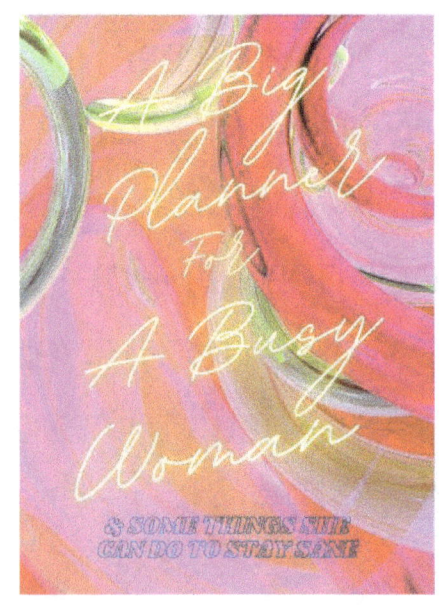

#Inspired Planner/Journal

Blank 18-month calendar/to-do lists/journal planner. Great for those quick thoughts, ideas, & late-night restless mind sessions.
Always be #Inspired
For everyone.

The ones who are crazy enough to think they can change the world, are the ones who do.

STEVE JOBS

www.ingramcontent.com/pod-product-compliance
Lightning Source LLC
Chambersburg PA
CBHW080909230426
43665CB00018B/2551